ANIMAL ARMIES

ANT COLONIES

RICHARD AND
LOUISE SPILSBURY

PowerKiDS
press.

New York

Published in 2013 by The Rosen Publishing Group, Inc.
29 East 21st Street, New York, NY 10010

Produced for Rosen by Calcium Creative Ltd
Editors for Calcium Creative Ltd: Sarah Eason and Katie Woolley
US Editor: Sara Antill
Designers: Paul Myerscough and Geoff Ward

Photo credits: Shutterstock: Stephane Bidouze 22r, BlankArtist 28–29, Fong Kam Yee 4–5, Kurt_G 26br, Injun 20b, Eric Isselée 6–7, Kuttelvaserova 24br, Henrik Larsson 8–9, 16–17, Nestor Noci 24–25, Noppasit TH 4br, Andrey Pavlov 1, 12–13, 18–19, 20–21, Michael Pettigrew 6r, Mikhail Hoboton Popov 16r, Dr. Morley Read 14–15, 18r, 22–23, Richard Schramm 14r, Shamleen 10br, Stevenku cover, 12b, SweetCrisis 10–11, Tan Hung Meng 26–27, Topten22photo 8br, Matt Valentine 28tr..

Library of Congress Cataloging-in-Publication Data

Spilsbury, Richard, 1963–
 Ant colonies / by Richard Spilsbury and Louise Spilsbury.
   p. cm. — (Animal armies)
 Includes index.
 ISBN 978-1-4777-0302-1 (library binding) — ISBN 978-1-4777-0326-7 (pbk.) —
ISBN 978-1-4777-0327-4 (6-pack)
 1. Ants—Behavior—Juvenile literature. 2. Insect societies—Juvenile literature.
I. Spilsbury, Louise. II. Title.
 QL568.F7S69 2013
 595.79'6—dc23

                          2012026320

Manufactured in the United States of America

CPSIA Compliance Information: Batch #W13PK2: For Further Information contact Rosen Publishing, New York, New York at 1-800-237-9932

CONTENTS

ANTS

Ants are small **insects**. They are usually colored yellow, brown, red, or black. Ants have six legs and two long **antennae,** or feelers, on their head. They use their antennae to feel and smell. Ants live almost everywhere on Earth, especially in hot places.

There are 10,000 different **species** of ants in the world. They live in many different **habitats**, from backyards and forests to deserts and mountains. All types of ants live in groups. Groups of ants are called colonies. There may be between 50 and hundreds of ants in one colony. Sometimes there can be as many as 10 million ants in just one colony! These are called supercolonies.

Ants are like a well-trained army. They work together as a team.

antenna

Some ants are as small as 0.08 inch (2 mm) long. The biggest ants are around 1 inch (25 mm) long!

Fight to Survive

Ants live in colonies so that they can survive. By working together ants can find food, care for their young, and **defend** their homes from attackers.

RANK

In an army, soldiers have different **ranks** and different jobs to do. In an ant colony, there are three ranks made up of queens, workers, and **drones**. The queen is the most important ant. She lays all of the eggs from which baby ants **hatch**. The queen ant is the mother of every single ant in the colony!

Most of the ants in a colony are workers, and they do all the work! They care for the queen and the young ants that hatch from her eggs. They collect food for the whole colony and also defend it from attack. All worker ants are adult females. Drones are always adult male ants. These ants leave their colony soon after they are born and live only for a very short time.

queen

The queen ant is easy to see. She is usually the biggest ant in a colony. Most colonies have one queen, but some have more.

Super Skills

Worker ants are very strong. Most can carry around 50 times their own body weight. Imagine trying to carry 50 friends on your back!

Worker ants must be strong to carry food and materials to make a home for the ants.

HOMES

Most colonies of ants live in nests underground. Other colonies live in nests above ground, made from materials such as twigs, sand, or stones. Worker ants build the nests. Sometimes they work together to dig out earth with their **jaws**. At other times they carry leaves and other materials to build the nest. After the nest is built, worker ants must repair it and keep it clean.

Inside a nest there are many tunnels that lead to many different rooms. The ant colony stores food in some of these rooms. Other rooms are used as bathrooms. The eggs and young ants are kept in rooms used as nurseries. The queen ant has her own room in the deepest part of the nest. Here, away from attackers, she can safely lay her eggs.

These worker ants are building a nest by gluing together grains of sand with their spit.

Super Skills

When army ants are on the move, they make living nests by linking their bodies together. They hold onto each other using hooks and spikes on their feet and jaws.

Colonies of wood ants pile pine tree needles and twigs above their underground nest. These anthills often have tunnels and rooms, too!

ON THE MOVE

Many worker ants leave their nest every day. These ants are called scouts. They leave to look for food to feed the other ants in their colony. After a scout finds food, it returns to its colony to ask other ants to help it carry the food back home. Back at the nest, the scout taps other worker ants to tell them to follow it back to the food.

Worker ants often travel a long way to find food. To help them remember the way back to the food, they leave a scent trail behind. As they walk along, they rub their **abdomen** on the ground, or on rocks and twigs. This leaves a smell behind. Other ants can then follow this smell between the nest and the food!

Ants from a colony follow a scent trail to get food.

These ants are working together to make a bridge for other ants to cross.

Fight to Survive

Some ants can make living bridges with their bodies. They hold onto each other to make bridges over puddles, holes in the dirt or rocks, and even gaps between plants.

FEEDING

Ants will eat almost anything! Many ants eat parts of plants. Some drink a sweet juice called **nectar** from inside flowers. Other ants suck sweet juices called **sap** from plant stems. Harvester ants collect grass, seeds, or berries to eat and store in the colony's nest.

Ants even eat small animals. Some ants eat eggs and young ants, which they steal from other ant nests. Ants work in teams to catch **prey**. First they surround the prey, so it cannot get away. Then the ants sting or bite the prey to kill it. Millions of army ants work together to catch prey. They hunt spiders, lizards, and snakes!

Sometimes prey is too big to carry back to the nest. The ants bite it into pieces and carry the pieces home.

Many ants eat the sweet, juicy parts of plants, such as the inside of a tomato.

Super Skills

Tree ants make traps on plant stems to catch prey. They shape the stem fibers into bridges. They leave holes in the bridge, then hide beneath them. When prey crosses the bridge, the ants jump up through the hole to grab it!

FOOD RATIONS

Worker ants share most of the food that they find. Ants carry liquid food back to the nest in their stomach. Their abdomen has two parts, a stomach and a **crop**. When ants find food, they swallow it. Some of the food goes into their stomach. This food is eaten by the ant. The rest of the food goes into the crop.

The food stored in the crop remains there until the worker ant returns to the nest. Then the ant spits up droplets of the food and passes it into the mouths of other ants. Worker ants feed other workers and the young ants in the nursery in this way. Hungry ants stroke the worker ant or tap it with their antennae to ask for food!

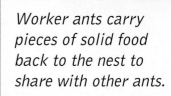

Worker ants carry pieces of solid food back to the nest to share with other ants.

Super Skills

Leafcutter ants bite off pieces of leaves and carry them back to the nest. There, they chew the leaves and put them into **fungus**. This helps more fungus to grow. The ants then eat the fungus.

Leafcutter ants carry pieces of leaf back to their nest.

NEW RECRUITS

Queen ants lay thousands of eggs during their lives. Some queen ants can lay one egg every few seconds! Once the queen has laid the eggs, worker ants take care of them. After a few days, **larvae** hatch out of the eggs. Larvae are young ants, but they do not look like ants. Instead they look like small, squirming white worms.

Worker ants feed the larvae to make sure that they grow. After a few weeks, the larvae are ready to change into adults. To do this most ant larvae spin a **silk** cover around themselves. This is called a **pupa**. After two or three weeks inside the pupa, the larva will have changed into an adult. The new **recruit** breaks out of its case and joins the colony.

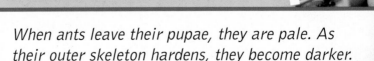

When ants leave their pupae, they are pale. As their outer skeleton hardens, they become darker.

Worker ants regularly check on eggs, larvae, and pupae to keep them safe and clean.

Who's Who?

The queen lives longer than any other ant in the colony. Queens live for around 5 to 30 years. Worker ants live for just a few months.

CARING FOR THE YOUNG

Caring for the young is a full-time job for some of the worker ants. There are several nursery rooms in the nest. Workers keep the eggs clean by licking them. If it gets too hot or too cold in a nursery, workers move the eggs, larvae, and pupae. Depending on the weather, they carry the young to rooms that are warmer or colder.

When it is time for ants to break out of their pupae, some are too weak to chew their way out. In these cases, the nursery workers help the baby ants by biting holes through the pupae. Young ants are pale and weak when they first leave their pupae. They cannot walk properly. Worker ants bring them food and care for them until they are ready to start work.

Worker ants gently hold eggs in their jaws to move them from room to room.

Workers bring food to new young adult ants to help them grow big and strong.

Super Skills

Weaver ants build their nests from folded leaves. Weaver larvae can make silk, so the workers pass the larvae along the leaves to glue, or weave, them together!

TALKING

Ants talk by passing messages to each other. They do this by giving off smells. They use these smells to lead other ants to food, warn them of danger, and to recognize if another ant is a friend or an enemy. Ants pick up these smells with their antennae.

Ants also talk to each other by making sounds. Some click their jaws together to make a sound. Carpenter ants and some tree ants make sounds by banging their head or antennae against a hard surface such as wood. The sounds send **alarm signals** to other ants in the colony. The ants feel and hear these sounds through their knees!

A fire ant gives off an alarm scent if it is in trouble. The scent tells other ants from the colony that it needs help.

Who's Who?

In some ant colonies, the queen does all the talking. She releases all the signals that tell ants in the colony what to do. Unfortunately, if the queen dies, the remaining ants do not know what to do!

When ants feed and lick each other's faces, they also put their smells on one another. When ants in a colony smell the same, they can easily recognize each other.

COLONY CHANGES

Once a year, queen ants lay eggs that hatch into males and young queen ants. Unlike the worker ants, these ants have wings. After hatching, they fly out of the nest and travel to meet males and young queens from other ant colonies.

Males and young queens **mate** in the air. Then the young queens find a place to start a new nest and a new colony. The males die. Other changes in the ant colony may take place, too. If the nest is damaged by an animal or fills with rainwater, the ants leave it. The worker ants carry the eggs, larvae, and pupae to a safe place. Then they immediately start to build a new nest.

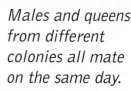

Males and queens from different colonies all mate on the same day.

If their nest is damaged, worker ants quickly carry eggs to safety.

Who's Who?

When a queen ant becomes old and dies, the colony can survive only for a few months. Without a queen to lay more eggs, the ant colony dies out.

ANT ENEMIES

Many different animals eat ants. Frogs, crickets, spiders, toads, birds, and lizards eat ants. Woodpeckers eat ants that make nests in the branches or trunks of trees. They peck holes in the wood with their sharp beaks and lick out the ants with their tongues. Chimpanzees sometimes even eat ants. They use sticks to scoop out ants from inside logs.

Giant anteaters tear open ant nests with their long claws. They then use their long, sticky tongue to scoop out the ants inside. Giant anteaters eat as many as 30,000 ants in one day, but they never destroy an anthill. They leave it standing so they can return to eat from it again.

When a nest is attacked, all the ants inside swarm out to protect it.

Inside the giant anteater's long snout is a tongue that is more than 2 feet (0.5 m) long. An anteater can flick its tongue 150 times a minute!

Who's Who?

Army ants work together in huge numbers to attack enemies. These great armies have few **predators**. Even the giant anteater will not battle with fearsome army ants!

DEFENDING THE COLONY

Worker ants fight for their colony. When ants see an attacker, they release alarm signals to call for help. Together the ants then fight the attacker. Using their jaws, they grasp enemies such as spiders and crickets and bite a hole in them. They then squirt poison into the wound from a stinger at the end of their abdomen.

Sometimes one colony of ants will attack another colony's nest. When this happens, worker ants from both sides fight each other. The ants from the winning colony steal the eggs from the losers' nest and take them to their own nest. The ants that hatch from the eggs do not become members of the new ant colony. Instead they become slaves.

A soldier ant uses its enormous jaws to fight enemies.

26

Ants attack and kill ants from other colonies that try to **invade** their nest.

Who's Who?

Some ant colonies have soldier ants. These ants have very big heads and huge, snapping jaws. Soldier ants use their big heads to block the entrance to the nest and keep out any intruders.

SURVIVAL

For every person on Earth, there are thousands of ants. Some are pests. Ants climb over people's food and eat it. They can tunnel into homes and lawns. People often use strong chemicals to kill ants that invade their homes. Yet, in some places, people eat ants and their eggs!

People may damage some colonies of ants, but ants are not in danger of dying out. There are billions of ants in the world. Ant colonies make eggs and young ants very quickly, so if an ant is killed, there are plenty to replace it. Ant colonies are amazing because they work together like well-trained armies. As a result, ants survive in many places all over the world.

Ants are small, but as a group they can achieve great things!

Ants quickly swarm over any left-behind food. They break it up into pieces to carry back to their nest.

Fight to Survive

For tiny ants, teamwork is a must! On its own, one ant would drown trying to cross a puddle. Together, ants link their bodies to make a raft and float over the puddle to safety.

GLOSSARY

abdomen (AB-duh-mun) The stomach area.

alarm signals (uh-LARM SIG-nulz) Signs that tell other ants something is wrong.

antennae (an-TEH-nee) A pair of feelers on an insect's head.

crop (KROP) Part of an animal or insect in which food is stored.

defend (dih-FEND) To protect against attack.

drones (DROHNZ) Male ants.

fungus (FUN-gis) Plantlike living thing.

habitats (HA-buh-tatz) Places where animals live.

hatch (HACH) To break out of a shell or protective covering.

insects (IN-sekts) Six-legged animals with three-sectioned bodies.

invade (in-VAYD) To break into something, or to try to take over.

jaws (JAHZ) Body parts that open and close the mouth.

larvae (LAHR-vee) A life cycle stage in which ants look like worms.

mate (MAYT) To reproduce, to make babies.

nectar (NEK-tur) A sweet juice found in the center of flowers.

predators (PREH-duh-terz) Animals that hunt other animals.

prey (PRAY) An animal that is eaten by other animals.

pupa (PYOO-puh) A stage in which an ant grows inside a covering.

ranks (RANKS) The positions within an army or a group.

recruit (rih-KROOT) A new member.

sap (SAP) A sugary liquid found inside plants.

silk (SILK) A sticky thread made by some animals.

species (SPEE-sheez) A type of animal.

FURTHER READING

Ashley, Susan. *Incredible Ants*. The Incredible World of Insects.
 New York: Gareth Stevens, 2012.

Dyer, Hadley, and Bobbie Kalman. *The Life Cycle of an Ant*.
 New York: Crabtree Publishing, 2006.

Stewart, Melissa. *Ants*. Des Moines, IA: National Geographic
 Children's Books, 2010.

WEBSITES

Due to the changing nature of Internet links, PowerKids Press has developed an online list of websites related to the subject of this book. This site is updated regularly. Please use this link to access the list: **www.powerkidslinks.com/aarmy/ant/**

INDEX